# ZODIAC Symbols

*Decoding the ancient symbology of the Zodiac*

Ruth Hadikin

# CONTENTS

# INTRODUCTION

The subject of Zodiac signs is one that has fascinated astrology lovers for generations, yet little is known about the ancient origin and meaning of the symbols and glyphs that we use in everyday astrology.

My own love of the Zodiac began long before I had ever heard of astrology or knew anything about it. When I was a child my grandfather gave me a wall poster that showed the Zodiac signs and glyphs for the different seasons of the year. I pinned it up by my bed and would fall asleep literally gazing at the stars! As I wondered about these mysterious symbols, who knows what magical and mysterious realms they transported me to as I slept.

As I grew older and learned more about astrology and the meaning of the Zodiac I never lost that sense of magic, and the feeling that the symbols themselves are conveying much more, beyond words.

This book is the result of my lifelong interest and many years of research into the deeper meaning of the Zodiac symbols and glyphs. Even now I feel as though we have barely scratched the surface of this mysterious topic, and that the Zodiac signs have so much more wisdom to impart than we are currently capable of understanding. In this book we delve into the history of astrology, exploring the ancient origins of the symbols that we use to represent Zodiac signs today.

The meaning of much symbology has unfortunately been lost in the mists of time, and we can only speculate on what the original meaning may have been for ancient people and their cultures.

For this reason some chapters in this book are necessarily longer than others simply because there is more information, both historical and mythological, surrounding some Zodiac signs than others. (Or at least those that we are aware of based on the myths and stories that have survived to the current time).

Before reading further it might be helpful to clarify some terms, particularly what we mean by a symbol and a glyph because, although these two terms are often used interchangeably, they are not the same thing.

A *symbol* is anything we use *to represent something else*. So if we say x equals ten, then the number ten is being symbolized by the letter x. In this example, the letter x is a symbol for ten.

Glyphs, on the other hand, are *pictorial images* that are used to symbolize something. So even though Glyphs are a *type* of symbol, you can also have a symbol that is not a glyph.

Take the Zodiac sign of Taurus, for instance. Taurus is *symbolized* by a Bull and this is sometimes represented by the *glyph* that is a circle with what appears to be 'horns' coming out of the top.

You could just as easily *symbolize* Taurus with a picture of a bull. That would be a symbol, but not a glyph. Using this example we can see how all astrology glyphs are symbols, although not all astrology symbols are glyphs.

People sometimes refer to astrological *glyphs* as

*sigils* but this is not technically accurate because sigils are something else entirely. Originally sigils were diagrams used by alchemists that were imbued with magical powers (often used as talismans) for specific purposes and outcomes.

There could be an argument that astrology glyphs may have originally been used as sigils at times, *if* they were imbued with the actual energy that they represent (by someone who had the power and capacity to do this). Since this is not generally the case in our modern era, it would be technically incorrect to refer to astrology glyphs as sigils, unless they have been imbued with such power and are being used for that purpose.

The word Zodiac comes from the ancient Greek word *zodiakos* which literally meant *circle of little animals*, it has it's roots in the word *zoion* which meant *animal* and was also the root of the modern word *zoo*.

The Zodiac is the name we give to a region of the sky, like a wide belt, based on how the Sun appears to travel across the sky over the course of a year, from our viewpoint on Earth. This apparent belt is divided into twelve sections that we call the Zodiac signs[1].

There is often some confusion between the twelve Zodiac signs and constellations that share the same name. Zodiac signs are not the same as constellations. This is discussed more in the chapter on the symbology of Libra.

Finally, I hope you enjoy this journey into the ancient world of awe, myth, and wonder, that comprises Zodiac symbology.

---

[1] Different astrological traditions use different Zodiac systems. The Tropical Zodiac is based on the changing seasons while the sidereal Zodiac is based on constellations.

# ♈

# ARIES

The symbol for Aries is the Ram. Aries is the first sign of the Zodiac and that in itself is symbolic: it is *the* sign of pioneering leadership. Aries is associated with inspiration, initiation, innovation, boldness, courage, impulsiveness and spontaneity. Going first, taking the initiative, pushing forward, and pushing through obstacles, are all key Aries themes.

No surprise then that *Aries Symbol* is the ram (the name 'Aries' is actually the Latin word for ram, battering ram, beam or prop). The battering ram was a contraption used in ancient and medieval warfare to 'push through' and break down an opponent's defenses.

When the Sun is at 0° of Aries it is the astrological point of Spring Equinox and the beginning of the astrological year. The *Aries symbol* therefore represents change, the energy of pushing through, moving forward, spring, new life, and new cycles.

## The Glyph for Aries

The glyph for Aries – a single line that divides into two – looks similar to the horns of a ram, but it also looks like a new shoot that has broken through the surface of the earth in spring, ready to burst into life.

Indeed, every spring as new life bursts forth, millions of tiny new seedlings are themselves like little battering rams in their journey from deep in the earth to their new life above ground!

The immense force these tiny, tender, shoots display as they push their way up through the earth, overcoming all obstacles such as rocks and tree roots in their mission to reach the light, is symbolic of the journey of Aries.

## Aries - Symbol of Existence

Aries is the sign of existence itself and in *Esoteric Astrology* it is said to be the sign that is 'closest to God'. In fact, in Esoteric Astrology, Aries is described as a *'point of light in the mind of God'*.

Aries is the first spark of creation, the original concept that manifests into form from the realm of the formless and is very much associated with ideas and concepts themselves.

As the Cardinal Fire sign, Aries is very much associated with inspiration and intuition and part of the spiritual purpose of Aries is to inspire others with Divine ideas.

Some of the qualities associated with Aries are those associated with spring: boldness, courage, inspiration, new ideas, pioneering, forging ahead and overcoming obstacles.

Aries can be a driving force behind new initiatives, and their ability to clear obstacles out of the way can be a breath of fresh air as they create the space for something new to manifest into existence.

There aren't as many different symbols associated with Aries as there are with some other signs (such as Scorpio for example). Such simplicity and directness is itself characteristic of Aries.

That said, don't be fooled by appearances. The simplicity of Aries belies the raw, direct, power of Nature herself, and when it comes to initiating a new project or idea Aries can be a force to be reckoned with. Indeed the ram itself is a symbol of power and force.

## The Ram in Ancient Greece and Egypt

Because of its association with power and fertility, the ram was a sacred animal in many ancient cultures. Ancient Greek mythology tells the story of how the god of the Sea, Poseidon, took the form of a ram to sire a winged ram with a golden fleece.

Later the goddess Nephele appeared in the form of the golden winged ram to carry her son Phrixus (who was due to be sacrificed) to safety. In return Phrixus returned the ram to Poseidon by sacrificing him, whereupon the ram became the constellation Aries.

Even earlier in history, in ancient Egypt, sacred rams were often kept as temple animals. We can see rams depicted frequently in ancient Egyptian art: at Karnak temple in Luxor (ancient Thebes) there is an avenue of rams leading to the entrance to the temple, and many ancient Egyptian gods are either depicted as having ram's horns or even a ram's head.

Interestingly the name of one of the most powerful Egyptian Pharaohs, *Ram*eses, means *"born of Ra"*. Ra means the source, or 'supreme God' so the name Rameses means *one who is born from the supreme source.*

Here again we have echoes of the esoteric theme of Aries, which is that of the first point of existence, arising from source or the void. From this we can see that the deepest spiritual symbology of *Aries represents the emergence from Divinity into existence.* In Christianity this sacred symbolism lives on in references to Christ as the *Lamb of God.*

Aries creates the space to exist. As the ultimate symbol of spring, creation and new life, Aries represents the power of the Divine life force energy itself, pouring into existence from a single point (or source).

If we look closely we might even see in the glyph of Aries, a resemblance to a water spout: a fountain of Divine energy, or life, spouting into existence from it's single Divine source.

# TAURUS

The symbol for Taurus is a bull. Taurus is associated with beauty, sensuality, and an artistic nature. Other Taurean characteristics include steadfastness, strength, hard work, patience, dependability, and stubbornness! Taurus rules the neck, shoulders, the throat, voice, and the throat chakra in the body.

Taurus is the *fixed earth sign* and is probably the most down to earth of Zodiac signs. That said, there is also a deeply spiritual side to this sign. Esoterically Taurus is associated with the opening of the third eye and with enlightenment.

*"I see and when the eye is opened, all is light"*

-The Tibetan, Esoteric Astrology

Buddhist Astrologer Jhampa Shaneman[2] thinks that the Buddha may have had six planets in Taurus. No surprise then that this sign has a strong association with illumination and spiritual awakening.

## The Constellation of Taurus

It's commonly believed that the *Taurus Symbol* comes from the constellation of Taurus. The stars are thought to form the shape of a bull's head and forequarters. But when you look at it, it isn't easy to see the shape of a bull. So the *Taurus symbol* possibly represents something much deeper than a mere visual similarity.

The constellation of Taurus is very large with two well-known star clusters: the Hyades and the Pleiades. The brightest star in Taurus

---

[2] *Buddhist Astrology (Chart Interpretation From A Buddhist Perspective)* by Jhampa Shaneman and Jan V. Angel.

is the red giant Aldebaran. It's name comes from the Arabic word *al-dabarān*, which means *the follower*.

Aldebaran is also called *the eye of the Bull*. In the Ancient Mystery schools this was called *the eye of illumination*. The reference to 'followers' and 'illumination' are another hint at a deep connection between Taurus and a path of spiritual awakening.

## Taurus Symbol in Esoteric Astrology

In *Esoteric Astrology* our soul's journey is said to begin in Aries as *a point of light in the mind of God*. In Taurus that point of light then becomes a single emanating *beam* of light. Accordingly, the energy of Life *takes shape* by moving *into form* in Taurus.

Taurus is the *fixed earth sign*. The earth element represents *substance*. In other words, the physical realm. In addition, 'fixed' energy forms structures: conduits, supports or containers.

Consequently the *esoteric purpose of Taurus is to maintain an unswerving single-pointed focus on the material plane.* Especially at this crucial early stage of our Soul's journey, when Life is moving outward on it's journey into form. In short, the esoteric purpose of Taurus is to be a steadfast guiding light.

*"The four cardinal signs mark the beginning of a season. These are Aries (spring equinox), Cancer, Libra (autumn equinox) and Capricorn.*

*Next, the four fixed signs mark the peak of each season. Taurus is the fullness of spring. Leo is the height of summer. Scorpio is the peak of autumn and Aquarius marks the depths of winter.*

*Finally four mutable signs mark the changing seasons. In Gemini spring rolls into summer. Virgo watches summer turn into autumn. Sagittarius rolls autumn into winter and in Pisces winter rolls into spring.*
*(These are the seasons in the Northern Hemisphere)."*

- (this author) in
*The Complete Foundations of Soul Astrology*

## The Energetic Qualities of Taurus

The *Taurus Symbol* of a bull probably represented energetic qualities. For instance, strength, endurance, single-mindedness, and a placid, gentleness of spirit.

## Bulls as Symbols of Fertility and Virility

One 'earthy' facet of Bull symbology is conception. In the sexual act, the 'seed of life' (represented by Aries) is symbolic of the creation of sperm.

The 'canal' of fixed energy (Taurus) is symbolic of the erect phallus. As a result, the 'seed of life' is directed, guided, and ejected into physical form by the energy of Taurus.

The Bull therefore symbolizes a male's capacity to father children. As a result many traditions of bull worship emerged throughout the ancient world.

Some were blatant celebrations of male power demonstrated by killing a Bull, for example in the Ancient Roman cult of Mithras. In contrast, other traditions viewed Bulls as sacred and they were protected.

## The Sacred Bull in Ancient Times

Taurus is thought to be one of the first constellations to be represented by an animal symbol. It was probably used in early forms of astrology to predict the best seasons for planting and sowing.

Cave paintings dating back 17,000 years or more, appear to show Taurus with the seven stars of the Pleiadies. It's also thought that by around 4,000 -1700 BCE Taurus marked the beginning of the 'new' year at spring.

## Timeline of Bull and Cow Worship through the Ages

- **c. 8,000 BCE.** Preserved ancient bull skulls were found at a sanctuary in **Anatolia** (Turkey).
- **3,300 BCE – present.** Bulls were featured on the seals of the **Indus Valley Civilization.** They were probably early forms of the current saivite deity Nandi. Cows and bulls are

not worshipped in the Hindu religion, but they are considered sacred and would not be killed or eaten.

- **3,000 BCE.** The Ancient **Sumerian** myth about a *bull of heaven* probably refers to the constellation of Taurus.
- **3,050 BCE – 400 CE** the Ancient **Egyptians** worshiped Apis the sacred bull. Worship of Apis as a deity is thought to have continued beyond the Egyptian empire, into ancient Greece and then Rome. The ancient egyptian goddess Hathor was also said to appear in the form of a cow.
- **2,700 – 1450 BCE** Ancient **Minoan** (Crete) artwork depicts people ceremoniously leaping over bulls, possibly in some kind of fertility rite.
- **1,200 BCE – 600 CE**. In **Ancient Greece** bulls were connected to the gods Zeus and Dionysus and to the goddess Hera. The Greek myth of the Minotaur featured a man with the head of a bull.
- **200-400 CE.** The **Romans** believed that ritually sacrificing bulls would benefit both the people and the state.
- **100-400 CE.** The Roman mystery cult of Mithraism also featured the ritual

slaying of bulls.

- **3,000 BCE – present day.** Bullfighting as a sport may have originated in ancient Mesopotamian religious rituals. From there it is thought to have spread across mediterranean cultures, including Spain. Cows are still considered sacred in India.

## The TAURUS Glyph

Taurus is *represented* by a *glyph* composed of a *semi-circle* on top of a *circle*. This appears to represent a bull's head, with two horns, but there are possibly much deeper meanings hidden in this simple glyph.

### The Circle and The Moon in the Taurus Symbol

Our modern calendar is a *solar* calendar, based on the Earth's orbit around the Sun. However, many ancient cultures used *lunar* calendars, based on the Moon's phases, to determine optimum times for planting crops. Therefore, the Moon was more meaningful to them than the Sun.

In astrology, the Moon is exalted in Taurus.

This means her energy is most active and able to flow freely. The Taurus glyph may be a simple symbol of the Moon. The full circle could symbolize the Full Moon. A semi-circle would represent a crescent Moon (see image).

This means the Taurus glyph could possibly have been a very simple symbol of the Moon and her phases.

## Taurus Symbol and the Throat

Some scholars have proposed that the Taurus glyph could be a symbol of the throat. In this theory the circle is thought to represent the throat itself while the bull's 'horns' would be the two *Eustachian* tubes that connect the throat and ears. Astrology Symbol specialist Fred Gettings explains:

*"it has been suggested that this is a vestigial drawing of the larynx, with the Eustachian tubes. The sigil thus*

*linking the ideas of **speech** and **hearing**.*

*This has been used as an explanation as to why the image of the bull is sometimes linked with Christ. For within both Taurus and Christ are contained the idea of the **logos** or '**Word**'. As well as the idea of blood sacrifice ...*

*in common with the other three fixed signs of the Zodiac, Taurus is linked with the Tetramorph and specifically with the Evangelist Luke."*

- Fred Gettings
*The Arkana Dictionary of Astrology*

## The Divine Circle

The circle in itself has deep symbolic meaning. Because it is without beginning and without end, it represents the infinite universe. In other words, it represents the unmanifested source from which all manifest reality arises.

*"God is a circle whose center is everywhere and circumference is nowhere"*

- Hermes Trismegistus

The circle in the Taurus glyph then, could also be interpreted as a symbol of unmanifest Divine potential. In addition, the 'horns' can be viewed as initial emanations of light into form.

Esoterically Taurus represents a path to enlightenment by releasing personal attachment. The patience, strength, and determination of a Bull is needed to overcome all obstacles on the path to spiritual awakening. Consequently, we can see just how perfect the Bull is, as a symbol for *Taurus*.

In conclusion, the esoteric purpose of the *fixed earth sign* (Taurus) is to be a *conduit for light* on it's journey into form.

Unlike other Zodiac signs that have many symbols, Taurus has only one: the Bull. This echoes and emphasizes the single-pointed purpose of Taurus.

# GEMINI

The symbol for Gemini is the *heavenly Twins*. Gemini is the first sign of the Zodiac to feature humans rather than animals in it's symbology. This is an early hint at Gemini's esoteric connection with the spiritual evolution of humanity.

The sign of Gemini is about connection, communication and communion. Esoterically, we noted earlier that the Soul begins it's journey in Aries as a point of light in the mind of God. This single point projects out as beam of light in Taurus, before fanning out to become myriad rays of rainbow light in Gemini, *touching all of existence.*

The light of Gemini seeks wisdom and, ultimately, resolves all extremes, polarities, and duality back into one, but first Gemini must fully experience the human journey, in order to gain wisdom.

The sign of Gemini is therefore about multiple experiences at the personality level, that contribute to learning, and finally transcending the ultimate duality: personality and Soul, to live as a Soul-centered being.

Gemini's symbology tells us much about the journey of light of the human Soul, and the evolution of consciousness. In other words, the Gemini symbol is hinting at *what it really means to be human.*

Astrology uses symbology to point to an underlying energetic reality. In the constellation of Gemini (which gave it's name to the Zodiac sign Gemini) the two brightest stars are Castor and Pollux.

## The Heavenly Twins: Castor and Pollux

Greek mythology often uses metaphor to point to the deeper meaning of our spiritual journey and experience. In the ancient Greek myth, Castor and Pollux were half brothers sharing the same mother but having different fathers.

Castor's father was mortal, and so was he. Pollux however was the son of the god Zeus, and so he was immortal. When Castor died, Pollux didn't want to lose his brother and asked Zeus to intervene. Zeus turned them both into stars so they could remain together forever as the *heavenly twins* in the constellation of Gemini.

The esoteric symbology is that each of us has a mortal self, which dies, and an immortal self (Soul), which is eternal. The journey of Gemini is one of experiencing the opposites of self and other, head and heart, personality and Soul, mortal and immortal, so that we eventually recognize our immortal self through our own personal experience.

The Heavenly Twins are symbolic of the two aspects of human nature: the Soul, which is immortal, and the personality, which will die.

The dominant dynamic of Gemini is the call of the Soul vs the pull of the personality. The urge is to seek, in order to seek knowledge, understanding, and wisdom but this innate curiosity can keep us from the very wisdom that we seek by constantly engaging us in worldly activities.

The innate curiosity of Gemini that is constantly looking outwards seeking novelty, must eventually be turned inward to be transformed into wisdom-seeking, which leads to deep inner truth.

## The Glyph of Gemini

The glyph for Gemini is the Roman numeral for two (II). The two pillars symbolize the inherent duality of worldly existence. We all live in duality until we walk the spiritual path that leads us to fully realize oneness or non-duality.

## A Portal of Opportunity

Between the two pillars we might also see a portal, inviting us to step between the two pillars and go beyond, thereby beginning our spiritual quest. By transcending the pillars of duality and form we begin our spiritual journey into directly perceiving our essential non-dual formless nature.

Inherent then, in the glyph of Gemini, is the concept of choice: on this side of the portal is mortality, duality and worldly existence, on the other side of the portal is immortality, oneness, and Divine existence.

The two pillars of Gemini symbolize a heavenly portal to our Soul's journey: an opportunity to go beyond worldly existence, if we take it. If we choose wisely then immortality and the truth of our spiritual nature awaits: if we choose to follow wisdom rather than the worldly pursuits of our ego.

Gemini is the mutable (changeable) air sign, and air signs are about the mind. This tells us that the portal in Gemini is about an *orientation of mind*. This is in contrast to the "Great Gates" of Cancer and Capricorn, which are also referred to in Esoteric Astrology. (We will discuss these more in the following chapter on Cancer).

The Great Gates of Cancer and Capricorn refer to actual *births* or *incarnations*, into realms of physical and spiritual existence repectively, whereas the portal of Gemini is a *faculty of attention* that focuses on a path that will either result in a spiritual rebirth (Capricorn) or a worldly incarnation (Cancer).

The sign of Gemini is known for it's 'magpie' nature: being curious and following the next novelty that captures one's attention. The lesson in Gemini is to learn, of all the phenomena that compete for our attention, which ones are likely to lead to greater spiritual development and evolution.

The portal in Gemini is about the power of *choosing where we place our attention,* rather than allowing ourselves to be blown about on the winds of change.

> *"He and the Teacher saw the third great Gate,*
> *opening before the son of man,*
> *revealing a new chance to tread the Way."*

- The Tibetan
*The Labours of Hercules: An Astrological Interpretation*

Gemini is symbolic of the great spiritual quest that our entire human family will undertake, sooner or later. It is the search for the deepest truth of our being: the search for our Soul; the search for light, for unity, for divinity, for instruction, and the ultimate wisdom.

## The Divine Messenger

As the Divine messenger, Gemini reminds us that we *are* a Soul, and in our everyday activities we shouldn't lose sight of our Divine Self, but rather try to integrate it into all our thoughts, words and actions.

Ultimately Gemini is reminding us that our personality will one day wane and 'die' and that it is our Soul, which is waxing and growing, that will go on beyond the death of this current life.

Gemini reminds us what it really means to be human: to undertake the human journey with awe and reverence. To seek and find our true nature and not to be distracted by worldly pursuits. To not be attached to our 'waning' self, the personality nature, which is transient and temporary, but to seek and find our 'eternal' self, our immortal twin, that has always been with us throughout the ages, and throughout countless incarnations.

# CANCER

The symbol for Cancer is a Crab. The sign of Cancer is associated with home, and crabs are known for carrying their home (their shell) wherever they go, but there is much more to the sign of Cancer than this.

The symbology of a protective shell also indicates that there is something very precious hidden within a container. Indeed, the theme of keeping something 'hidden' is very important in Cancer, because this sign represents the deepest mysteries of Life, which are always hidden from the unenlightened simply because we don't yet have the capacity to perceive them.

Of the twelve constellations that share their name with Zodiac signs, Cancer is considered the 'quietest', in that there are no bright stars to attract attention.

The Zodiac sign of Cancer is also strongly associated with nurturing and birth and esoterically Cancer is associated with incarnation into a human life.

Our human journey into this Earthly Life begins in the protective safety and nurturing waters of our Mother's womb.

Esoterically, as the cardinal water sign, the sign of Cancer provides a vital realm of experience in the human Soul journey through the Cardinal Cross[3]:
*creation* (Aries);
*manifestation* (Cancer);
*legislation* (Libra) and
*initiation* (Capricorn)

Deep within the symbology of Cancer, the deepest mysteries of manifestation and Life

---

[3] For more explanation of the esoteric meaning of the four points of the Cardinal Cross see *Esoteric Astrology* by Alice Bailey.

itself lie hidden, awaiting our discovery: the actual process of how sentient beings, particularly human beings, *manifest* into physical Life forms.

### Scarab, Crayfish, Crab

Our modern symbol of a crab for Cancer is relatively recent. In medieval times Cancer was represented by a *crayfish*, and in ancient Egypt, by a *scarab* (dung beetle). All three creatures have a hard outer shell, within which the delicate processes of Life can unfold undisturbed.

The scarab or dung beetle was regarded with great reverence by the ancient Egyptians as it's vital role in the continuation of Life was recognized.

Realizing that the sign of Cancer represented the most sacred processes of Life, a sacred animal was adopted as it's symbol.

Later in history the scarab fell out of favor as it's association with dung came to be regarded as unclean by later societies.

Only recently, as our knowledge of the vital importance of healthy soil and the role of the microbiome[4] grows, are we beginning to understand the true role of the dung beetle in providing vital nourishment, for the health of the planet and the continuation of Life on Earth.

The significance of Cancer cannot be underestimated and the symbol of the Scarab, the sacred dung beetle, should be emblazoned in our minds as a symbol of rebirth and Earth's healing.

By medieval times the symbol for Cancer had been replaced with a crayfish, and later by our modern symbol of a crab, but nevertheless both animals are known to be scavengers and therefore play an important role in cleaning up their environment by removing debris and transforming it into precious Life.

All the symbols for Cancer therefore play a vital role in the *cycle of Life*.

———————————————

[4] The microbiome is the ancient population of microscopic organisms, including viruses and bacteria, that have inhabited the Earth since long before the arrival of humans. They are considered vital to the continuation of Life on Earth.

## Emotional Intelligence and Mandala Principle

Hidden even deeper within Cancer's symbology is the esoteric mystery of how forms (particularly human beings) actually exist.

As the cardinal water sign, Cancer is associated with emotions and emotional intelligence, and is ruled by The Moon.

Esoterically The Moon is known as *the Mother of all forms*. Here we have a hint at the mysterious connection between emotions and form.

In his book *Never Turn Away*, Buddhist Lama Rigzin Shikpo explains how everything in existence, exists by way of *Mandalas* (fields of energy and experience). He says that human emotions *form the boundaries* of human mandalas.

So therein lies a deep esoteric principle: human mandalas (realms of human experience and existence) are *held in place by human emotions*. In order to understand that we need a much deeper awareness of emotions than is commonly understood.

## Information is Light

Emotions are information, and information is carried on Light. This means that our emotional tendencies can be carried forward, in the Light of our being, to our next rebirth, and thereby shape our experience.

This is why the sign of Cancer is associated with mothers, birth, and the mysterious processes of gestation and embryology: the mysterious process of how *all forms come to be birthed into existence in order to be a vehicle for a specific realm of experience.*

The simple crab with it's precious cargo of Life-force energy encased within a protective shell is the symbol for this entire mysterious process of existence. To fully understand the symbolism of the crab we need to fully understand what Rigdzin Shikpo calls mandala principle[5].

Mandala principle is the name given to both the *process* whereby our continued thoughts and emotions generate fields of experience and the existence or *form* of those energy fields

---

[5] *Never Turn Away: The Buddhist Path Beyond Hope and Fear* by Rigdzin Shikpo

themselves.

## The Great Mystery of Existence

Hidden deep within the mysteries of Cancer, is the mystery of Life itself: the Great Mystery of how living things manifest into physical form.

The signs of Cancer and Capricorn are known esoterically as *The Great Gates*, of which Cancer is the Gate into physical existence and Capricorn is the Gate into Spiritual existence. (This is in contrast to the portal in Gemini that we mentioned in the previous chapter, which is an *orientation of mind* rather than a physical manifestation).

## Cancer Glyph

We can see a similarity in the Cancer glyph to two embryonic life forms. For mammals in general, and humans in particular, Life begins as an embryo in the safety of a womb, the precious container within which the mysteries of life unfold. The Cancer glyph may represent two embryonic life-forms.

## The Journey of Light into Form

At a deeper level the Cancer glyph could also be symbolic of the journey of *Light into form*. Esoterically it is said that we are beings of light. Modern research is now supporting this fact with the discovery that we have our own innate light, and that our DNA emits light.

It is now thought that messages are transmitted throughout our body, via the nervous system, with light. In effect our nervous system is like a fibre optic network for the reception and transmission of light. In early embryonic development, this 'network of Light' (our nervous system) begins as a tiny tube of light called the neural tube.

Neurobiologists tell us that this tube becomes our spinal cord and that one end of the tube bulges to form our brain. The Cancer glyph could therefore also represent this stage of embryonic development, where the brain is emerging from the spinal cord and, as such, could symbolize *the beginning of the journey of Light into form*.

Many of the activities associated with the Cancer symbol are those that involve the process of manifesting, nurturing, and supporting, Life on Earth. This includes gestation and birth: the development of a 'home' or container (womb), creating a field of energy that can nurture and sustain the growth of an embryo; keeping the environment safe and free from harm; immersion in water; and eventual birth.

When we fully understand the secrets of Cancer symbology we will know the deep hidden mysteries of the womb; how beings come into existence in physical form; how human realms of experience are generated and exist as Mandalas (fields of energy); and what determines birth into the human realm and the entire mandala of human experience.

To truly realize the deepest symbology of Cancer is to know the mystery of Life itself.

# ♌

# LEO

The Leo symbol is a lion. As a symbol, the lion might appear to be the most obvious symbol for the sign of Leo: for thousands of years, in the human psyche, lions have been a symbol first and foremost of strength, followed closely by courage and pride. The Zodiac sign of Leo is associated with strength, courage, will, creativity, the heart, pride, and... ego!

Esoterically, ego symbolizes the stage of the Soul's development where the individual becomes aware of itself: so the path from self-awareness to self-realization is the Soul journey of Leo.

The process of ego formation, identification, recognition and finally dissolution, is an integral part of this journey. But what for? What lies beyond the dissolution of ego? The Leo symbol offers us a glimpse…

## Lion of Ages – Lion, Horse, Sphinx

Within the context of the *Great Astrological Ages* (each one lasting about 2,160 years), it was during the Ages of Leo that great creativity spread throughout humanity. Ancient people believed the first *Time of Creation* may have happened during a Leo Age.

## Sphinx

Some scholars speculate that the Great Sphinx of Egypt may originally have been a Lion, and that the Lion's head eroded over time and was later refashioned into a pharaoh's head. The building of the sphinx is thought by some to coincide with the last age of Leo that took place between 10,500 BC to 8000 BC.

*"Great Sphinx is gazing directly DUE EAST, whereas the constellation of Leo rose at that time some 28 degrees north of due east. The correct epoch for the Great Sphinx to gaze at his own image would be 10,500 BC …*

*what makes the Sphinx-Leo correlation of 10,500 BC unlikely to be a coincidence is that it 'works' in conjunction with the 'beginning' of the Precessional cycle of Orion's belt as seen in the southern sky, which can be matched on the ground with the Giza Pyramids.*

*This 'beginning' I have identified to the golden age that the ancients called Zep Tepi meaning the First Time (of creation)."*

- Robert Bauval[6]

In modern astrology the sign of Leo is ruled by The Sun. The link between Leo and the Sun can also be traced back to ancient Egypt. The ancient Egyptians believed that Leo (the Cosmic Lion) was an aspect of the Sun God, Ra.

Richard H. Wilkinson, professor of Egyptology at the University of Arizona, and

---

[6] Robert Bauval is a researcher and writer on alternative history. His website is RobertBauval.co.uk

an expert on Egyptian deities, writes:

*"An important mythological aspect of the solar god in the heaven is found in his identity as a cosmic lion as seen in Chapter 62 of the Book of the Dead, for example, which states that 'I am he who crosses the sky, I am the lion of Re...'*

*The stellar constellation now known as Leo was also recognized by the Egyptians as being in the form of a recumbent lion... the constellation was directly associated to the sun god."*

- Richard H. Wilkinson

The Sphinx was therefore likely to be a symbol of Leo, the Cosmic Lion, which in turn was considered to be an aspect of the Sun God Ra, and was built to mark a very sacred place and time: that of the first time of creation.

To this day, of all twelve Zodiac signs, the sign of Leo is still the one most associated with creativity.

### Horse

Lions have indeed symbolized strength and

power throughout the ages, yet another common symbol associated with power, is the horse.

Some scholars have suggested that in far ancient times the sign that we call Leo may have been represented by a horse, while it was the sign of Cancer that was represented by the lion. This is interesting since both signs are associated with different *stages of creation*.

*"they consider that it is likely that leopard or lion symbolism represents Cancer and see it therefore as one example of modern variation, in that "the feline symbol appears to have moved from Cancer to Leo" (they consider that Leo is likely to be represented by horse symbolism)."*

- Philip Jamieson[7]

## Esoteric Meaning

Esoteric texts teach that in the journey of Creation, three root energies emerged from Source (or God) to create all of manifest

---

[7] Dr Philip Jamieson is a retired former academic and researcher who writes about ancient cultures, mythology, animal welfare, spirituality and the environment. His blog is at https://innerscribe.home.blog

existence. These are love, wisdom, and will (or power). Of these three, Leo is most associated with *will*, and it is part of the spiritual path of Leo to learn *right use of will*, so that the power of will is used in service of the Divine and not the ego.

Leo symbolizes the journey of Self, through right use and application of will. This journey takes us through three stages:

- **self-consciousness** – the initial realization that we exist as a separate individual;
- **self-awareness** – where we realize our own nature and power. In this stage we realize the impact of our thoughts, words, and actions on other sentient beings and the world around us.
- **self-realization** – we become a fully awakened human being.

## Punya - Spiritual Power

The kind of strength that is symbolized by the lion of Leo is not physical strength like we would think of it in the ordinary sense of the word.

In Sanskrit there is a term *punya*, which refers to a kind of *spiritual strength or power*. It is an inner strength that comes when our heart's purest intentions are aligned with Divine Will, in the service of spiritual awakening. We might think of it as the sacred strength of heart connection.

When the esoteric teachings refer to the 'right use' of will they are pointing to the power of consciously expressing Divine Will through the heart, rather than the unconscious use of will to pursue egoic desires.

When we have transcended ego, and all our intentions are directed through a pure heart, with a sincere desire to be of benefit to all sentient beings, only then will we realize the full power of *punya*.

Making the transition from egoic will to sacred *punya*, is the spiritual journey of Leo. This is why the sign of Leo is associated with the qualities of creativity, will, and the heart. When all three are fully realized then the sacred power of punya will be fully awakened and active.

## Leo Glyph

The origin of the current Leo glyph is unknown. Some scholars have suggested it may be a corruption of the Greek letter "L" (Lambda, see image).

All astrological glyphs may be considered esoteric in origin and nature in the sense that they may represent spiritual truths that can only be accessed intuitively.

As with many esoteric symbols, the power of the glyph lies in it's ability to by-pass our conditioned mind and speak to us directly through intuition. It is by contemplating the glyphs that spiritual truth can be revealed to us.

In contemplating the glyph for Leo we can see a striking similarity to diagrams that quantum physicists use to illustrate a concept known as *particle-wave duality* (see image[8]).

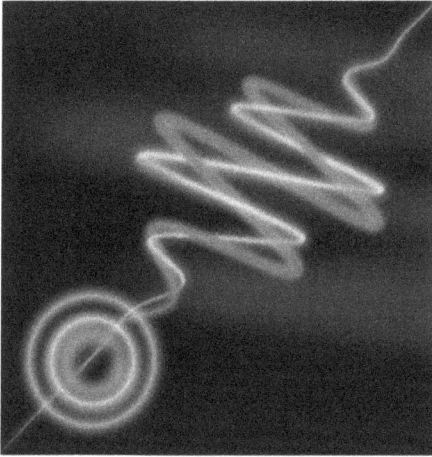

Particle-wave duality is a term used to describe how objects at the quantum level can exist as *both* a particle and a wave. As we look at the glyph for Leo, could it be that we are seeing a representation of a particle and a wave?

*"Quantum physics says that particles can behave like waves, and vice versa. Researchers have now shown that this 'wave-particle duality' is simply the quantum*

---

[8] Image Credit: Timothy Yeo / CQT, National University of Singapore

*uncertainty principle in disguise."*

> \- Timothy Yeo CQT,
> National University of Singapore

If the Leo glyph does represent a particle and a wave it would be a very appropriate symbol to convey the mysteries of creation that are hinted at within the Leo symbology.

Esoterically Leo is associated with creativity, will, and perhaps most importantly, Leo is a sign of the heart. Everything in creation exists in duality: self-other; male-female etc. Whether a quantum object exists as a particle or a wave is influenced by our intention, and 'right use' of our intention (will) happens only through the heart.

Ancient masters and yogis may not have used the term *particle-wave duality* but they had access to higher mind and the secrets of creation. Perhaps we could also say that the circle represents our personal mandala of self (our personal energy field centered in our heart), while the 'wave' represents our conscious intention flowing out into the world.

Either way, the Leo Glyph may be intended

to convey an intuitive message about the relationship between creation, right use of will (or intention), and the power of the heart.

## The Journey of Self-Realization

Esoterically, the sign of Leo also symbolizes the journey of human consciousness, through self-realization to being fully awakened as Soul-centered beings of light.

*"The German philosopher Friedrich Neitzche spoke of three stages of consciousness: the Camel, the Lion and the Child. The Camel represents tribal consciousness, where we follow the herd, follow the masses, and go along with the collective consciousness. The Camels are sleeping – no great awakening here! This is the pre-egoic state.*

*The Lion represents individualization – the ability and the willingness to stand alone. Separate. Apart from the herd. In terms of our personal spiritual development this is the development of, and identification with, our ego. The Lions (represented by Leo) are waking up. This is our currently emerging egoic state."*

- (this author) in
Life Coaching Magazine[9]

---

[9] *The Age of Aquarius: Evolving Consciousness.* Life Coaching Magazine, February 22 2016. Online article at

The process of Self-realization is one of spiritually awakening into higher and higher states of conscious awareness, until we become a fully awakened human being: fully aware of our nature as light, our power and capacity, and are fully Soul-centered with a deep motivation to be of benefit to all sentient beings.

Leo is a very important sign for our times: it represents the entire journey of humanity, from the first creation, to spiritual awakening and blossoming into beings of light, compassion, and higher consciousness.

During the coming Age of Aquarius (Leo's opposite sign) we will initially continue to be distracted by advanced technology. Right use of will happens only when we remain connected to our heart. Leo reminds us not to lose sight of our heart as we navigate these challenging times.

We all need the strength and courage of a Lion's heart.

---

https://lifecoachingmagazine.net/age-of-aquarius/

# ♍

## VIRGO

Virgo's symbol is a woman, often depicted holding an ear of corn or sheaf of wheat. Virgo is ruled by Mercury, the planet of the mind, and even though Virgo is an Earth sign (we usually associate air signs with mental activity) it is very much a sign that is committed to intellectual process.

When we think of how the Virgo mind works we can think in terms of analytical processing. Other Virgo themes include harvesting the fruits of our labor, purity, health, precision, discernment, method, practicality, and caring.

Virgo's genius lies in the practical application of information: using precision discrimination to determine what is useful, and what is not, and then cultivating practical techniques that can be of service to the greater good.

The downside of this kind of mind is over-thinking and 'analysis paralysis', which is a mental state whereby thinking itself becomes the end product and leads to a circular downward spiral of exhaustion without any resulting practical application.

When Virgo begins to feel exhausted they have very likely followed their thoughts down a dead-end or into a self-perpetuating thought-vortex that is leading nowhere.

The spiritual path of Virgo is to learn to apply discrimination to thought itself: to determine which thoughts will bear fruit – by leading to higher wisdom and virtuous action, and which thoughts are at best, fruitless and at worst, harmful to themselves and others.

This is where meditation for purification becomes important. It is Virgo's job to become a 'gardener' of their own mind, discriminating the weeds of negative thinking from the roots of wisdom.

## The Virgin

Virgo's symbol of a woman, is commonly assumed to be a virgin, holding a sheaf of wheat or an ear of corn, and often shown with wings indicating holiness, saintliness and/or spiritual maturity. The word *virgo* is Latin for virgin. Historically Virgo has also been associated with agriculture, fertility, and harvesting that which we have sown.

Virgo has been said to be a sign of both virtue and vice. The Latin word *vir*, which is the stem of virtue, means man, while the word vice means *to render ineffective*. The process of cultivating wise discrimination is vital to the journey of Virgo if we are to remain effective in our actions and not render ourselves ineffective.

In terms of our own spiritual awakening those actions which are most effective in supporting us are those that are virtuous, while those actions that are ineffective or create hindrances on our path, are those associated with 'vices' (temptations and repetitive habits that distract us from our path). It is in Virgo that we develop the art of discrimination, so we know which is which.

How can we know which actions will lead us to spiritual strength, and which will render us ineffective on our path? The myths of Virgo invite us to consider karma, and the idea that we will reap the fruits of all our actions, both positive and negative.

## Virgo in Mythology

In the various mythologies associated with Virgo we see a common theme in matters of life and death. The story of Icarius[10] is sometimes associated with Virgo: where Icarius recalls on his own deathbed, the circumstances that had led to his previously killing a goat.

Only on his own deathbed did he have the realization that in killing the goat, he had harmed himself. In Virgo's analysis of 'right

---

[10] In Greek mythology Icarius was the father of Erigone. Icarius is represented by the constellation Bootes, which borders Virgo, and Erigone is represented by Virgo.

action', karmic consequences also have to be taken into consideration if we are to see the full picture.

In *The Labours of Hercules*[11] the theme of karma is also played out in Hercules sixth labor: the labor of Virgo. In error, Hercules kills the Queen of the Amazons (the Latin word *virago* means man-like or warrior woman), because he failed to understand his mission. He is then cast out by his teacher until he can redeem himself, which he does by rescuing a maiden. In other words saving a life redeemed him for taking a life.

In the above myths of Virgo, both wrong and right action are taken, and their respective consequences experienced. In this way, through subsequent deaths and rebirths, the human journey gives each of us similar opportunities to cultivate greater discernment and wisdom, and experience the natural law of karma. In Virgo symbology the sheaf of wheat or ear of corn represents the fruit of our actions.

There is an apparent contradiction in the

---

[11] *The Labours of Hercules: An Astrological Interpretation* by Alice Bailey.

symbology of Virgo in that the Latin word virgo means *virgin*, while the sign of Virgo also symbolizes qualities such as bearing fruit, nurturing, and the wisdom of plant medicine.

In other words, Virgo is not only associated with virginity but is also associated with motherly qualities that are not usually associated with virgins. However, if we look to the deeper esoteric associations of Virgo this seeming contradiction begins to make more sense.

## Esoteric Meaning

The confusion in the myth of Virgo appears to be that Virgo means virgin, while the sign of Virgo also symbolizes maternal qualities.

This seems to be a logical paradox since virgins, in the literal sense, cannot be mothers. Yet if we explore this more we may come to an even deeper understanding of the meaning of the Virgo Symbol.

The word virgin not only applies to a young maiden, but is also used to refer to anything that is pure in terms of being *in it's natural state*.

For example, we may speak of virgin land, meaning land that has never been cultivated, so it remains in its natural state.

The sign of Virgo has had long associations with the Virgin Mary (Latin: Maria Virgo), or the Virgin Mother. On medieval paintings of the Virgin Mother and Child there is often depicted a star (on her dress or head) known as *Stellar Maris* (Star of the Sea), which is thought to represent the fixed star Spica in the constellation of Virgo.

In some schools of Tibetan Buddhism, there is a practice known as *The Great Perfection*, which is thought to be one of the highest teachings in Tibetan Buddhism. In the tradition of The Great Perfection the purpose is for the practitioner to recognize the natural state, within himself.

This involves deep meditative practices in which they develop a capacity for seeing their own mind in it's naked natural state, without any of the societal and familial conditioning that usually occupy our minds.

This process is often spoken of in terms of 'purification' and 'the perfection of wisdom'. It is said that once we 'purify' our minds of our everyday conditioning, we can experience our mind in it's natural state. In other words, we would experience a pure, or 'virgin', mind and that would be the highest of all wisdom.

Within the tradition of The Great Perfection, there is reference to the *Mother and Son*. In this case the Mother represents the void or Source: the purity from which all thought arises, and the Son represents the awareness that arises from Source. In other words, the 'Mother' Source gives 'birth' to the Son 'awareness'.

In Esoteric Astrology it is said that this 'Mother and child' symbology refers not just to the literal birth of the infant Jesus Christ, but to the stage at which we experience *Christ Consciousness* in our personal journey of spiritual awakening. It is also said that our spiritual journey truly begins in the sign of Virgo.

The planetary ruler of Virgo is Mercury, which relates to the mind, yet the Esoteric ruler is The Moon, which is the mother of all forms. In Esoteric Astrology, once again, we have an association between Virgo and Mother and Child symbology. Esoteric Astrology gives a

Soul keynote for each sign, which esoteric students are invited to contemplate, in order to inspire deeper insights. The Soul keynote for Virgo is:

*"I am the mother and the child.*
*I, God, I, matter am."*

This requires deep contemplation if we are to gain insight into the highest teachings inherent in the Virgo Symbol. The body of work known as *Esoteric Astrology* by Alice Bailey was transmitted telepathically by a master who was said to be abbot of a monastery in Tibet.

When it was first written, Buddhism was unheard of in the West, and there was limited access to accurate teachings on Tibetan Buddhist thought, especially in English. Now we have access to a great volume of Tibetan Buddhist teaching that has been translated into English, so we can more easily cross reference what the Tibetan may have been trying to teach through Esoteric Astrology.

One of the highest teachings in Tibetan Buddhism is the *Heart of The Perfection of Wisdom Sutra*, sometimes simply called The Heart

Sutra. In this text the Buddha gives a teaching to his disciples, that goes something like this:

> *Form is empty.*
> *Emptiness is form.*
> *Emptiness is not other than form.*
> *Form is also not other than emptiness.*
>
> — The Heart Sutra

In this context we might think of 'emptiness' as the void, or Source of all that is: that vast, formless, state of consciousness before form manifests. We could also think of it as God or the Divine. The Heart Sutra is giving a deep teaching on how forms come into being from the 'mind of God', are part of God and therefore can never really be separate. This is the essence of the Tibetan's keynote for Virgo: that mother, child, God, and matter are all one.

The drive to perfection is innate in Virgo however, discrimination is needed to know where to apply one's energy to be of the highest benefit to all. The deeper spiritual path of Virgo is about the perfection of true virtue (leading to spiritual strength) and the perfection of wisdom for the benefit of all sentient beings. In other words, the spiritual path of Virgo is the Great Perfection: the realization of our innate 'virgin' natural state, and the highest wisdom.

## The Virgo Glyph

The glyph for Virgo seems to have evolved from a graphic representation of a serpent. Earlier versions from ancient Greece and Egypt certainly look more serpent-like than our modern form.

In ancient symbology the serpent often represented kundalini, our innate sexual energy, life-force-energy, prana or chi. In contrast to Scorpio, whose glyph also seems to be derived from a serpent, the 'head' of the serpent in Virgo is lowered (in our modern form we may even say turned inwards) indicating, humility, piety and virtue. In the Greco-Roman and medieval periods, and even in many modern versions, the head appears to be severed completely, often indicated by a single stroke (see image: Variations in The Virgo Glyph).

This could symbolize the idea of taming our egoic urges or desires (the serpent), in order to

Variations in The Virgo Glyph
Ancient Egypt to Modern Day

| Demotic Script Ancient Egypt 7th - 5th Century BCE | Greco-Roman 8th century BCE - 6th century AD | Medieval 5th century AD -15th century AD | Modern |

<astrology-symbols.com>

cultivate greater virtue (or spiritual power).

In our modern version of the Virgo Glyph the 'head' turns back on itself forming a closed loop – a container in which such spiritual power may be stored. We might even interpret this to mean that we use our 'head', in other words the power of our own mind, to tame our lower urges and accumulate spiritual power.

In the previous chapter on the Leo Symbol we discussed the concept of *punya*, or spiritual power. This power is cumulative, and the practice of celibacy in certain spiritual traditions is associated with the intention to cultivate and build such spiritual power.

This idea of dedicating one's life-force energy to spiritual development is also a theme in Aquarius, but begins here in Virgo with the idea of discernment and consciously choosing which seeds we wish to plant, and which future spiritual 'crops' we wish to harvest.

We can also see from this example that Zodiac glyphs are not fixed in time, but rather they are adapted to reflect the understanding, knowledge, and consciousness of the times in which they are used.

When I look at the Virgo glyph I see roots: the roots of virtue and the roots of wisdom. Similar to the maiden's wings, this for me symbolizes the Virgo theme of bringing Divine energy down to earth and grounding it in practical ways!

It has also been suggested that the modern Virgo glyph was created by merging the letters *MV*, the initials of Maria Virgo, which is Latin for Virgin Mary.

## Virgo Symbol – The Great Perfection

In short, we can see that some definite themes emerge in Virgo Symbology to suggest the beginning of our path toward spiritual awakening.

We have the theme of discernment: where we cultivate the capacity to know which actions will be virtuous, in that they lead to greater spiritual strength or power, and those which would be non-virtuous (vice) because they would deplete our spiritual energy.

We have the theme of karma, where we learn the natural law of cause and effect. In other words, we reap what we sow.

Most of all we have the theme of purification of negative thoughts and the perfection of the wisdom mind, otherwise known as the Great Perfection.

In Virgo we take the concept of right will that was developed in Leo, and translate it into right action. In this way Virgo prepares and cultivates the ground in which the insights (or fruit) of our higher spiritual wisdom will grow.

## LIBRA

The symbol for Libra is the scales. The sign of Libra is associated with balance, harmony, ethics, relationships and beauty. Interestingly, Libra is the only sign of the Zodiac not represented by a living creature, and from an esoteric perspective is said to be one of the most difficult signs to understand.

The symbology of the scales seems obvious: when we think of scales we think of weighing things in balance, judgement, and justice. This is part of the symbology but as we shall see, when we dive into the deeper, esoteric, meaning of Libra, there is much more to this sign than meets the eye.

## The Scales

The Libra symbol has been associated with scales from earliest times. In ancient Babylonia the name for Libra was *Zibanitu*, which literally meant 'scales'. Indeed the Latin word Libra means scales, balance, or level.

There is so much confusion surrounding the symbology for the sign of Libra, that it might be helpful at this point to clarify the distinction between *signs and constellations*.

A *constellation* is a *pattern of stars*. They were given names in ancient times such as Aquila, Scorpius, and Pegasus. There are at least 50 major constellations and many minor ones. They are widely distributed across the northern and southern night sky and have never been described in terms of a wide 'band' or belt. Constellations vary greatly in size.

In contrast, the Zodiac divides the ecliptic (the Sun's apparent path around the Earth) into *twelve 30° arcs* known as *signs*, forming a *wide band* around the Earth. Although the twelve Zodiac signs share the same names as some constellations, they do not correspond in size or location.

Constellations often overlap, Zodiac signs do not. The twelve signs of the Zodiac are therefore equal in size because each occupies an equal 30° portion of the Zodiac belt[12].

It is important to remember this, especially when considering the myths of Virgo and Libra. For example one myth suggests that the woman in Virgo is the Greek Goddess Astraea, and that she holds the scales of Libra. Another suggests the claws of Scorpio are holding the scales of Libra.

While it is interesting to contemplate what this symbolism might mean, it is also important to keep in mind that these myths are referring to the *constellations*, and not the *Zodiac signs* of the same name.

This is important because the myth of the scales is often used to derive an interpretation of judgement and justice, which may be meaningful up to a point, but when we get to the deeper esoteric symbolism of Libra, the scales could mean something entirely different: that takes us beyond judgement and worldly

---

[12] Both Tropical and Sidereal Zodiacs have twelve equal signs. The exception is the True Sidereal Zodiac, which aligns more closely with constellations.

ideas of 'justice'.

The scales of Libra are sometimes depicted tilted to the right and are not necessarily balanced. This could reflect Libra's underlying spiritual path of continually turning toward that which is right, or in harmony. In other words, that which is in *right relationship* with all that is.

## Equanimity

The Sun enters Libra at Autumn equinox, one of the two occasions each year when the day and night are of equal length. For this reason the sign of Libra is associated with balance.

However, from an esoteric perspective Libra not only invites us to restore balance in our daily lives but also to explore the deeper universal law of harmonics that is arrived at through right relationship.

*"Harmony exists wherever there is right relationship. For example, in music there can be 'consonant' (congruent) sounds and dissonant (incongruent) sounds. Contrary to popular belief*

*harmony doesn't happen only when there are consonant sounds, but where there is a balance between consonant and dissonant sounds."*

- (this author) in
*Soul Astrology: How Your Rising Sign Reveals Your Soul Path and Life Purpose*

To understand how right relationship leads to harmony we can use the example of the musical scale. When notes are played randomly, we hear it as noise. We only hear music when there is some sort of order: in other words, when notes are played in right relationship to one another we hear rhythm, melody and music.

Whatever field we are in, it is the *relationship* between the individual component parts that give a sense of harmony or beauty. Understanding the universal law of right relationship is one of the esoteric themes of Libra.

This leads to another Libra theme, that of choice. The art of choice: knowing when and where to place our attention, is a major theme in Libra. On a worldly level it leads to the study and application of ethics, where we learn the art and science of how to make better choices.

On an esoteric, or spiritual, level the art of choosing where to place our attention moment by moment, is part of deeper yogic practices that can lead to full spiritual awakening.

One of the stages that yogis can experience through this process is known as equanimity or calm abiding. This is where the practitioner has fully developed the capacity to rest calmly in his own being, irrespective of what is happening around him. No longer tossed around by the constantly changing events of the outside world, they are able to remain at peace within themselves.

In Esoteric Astrology the Tibetan Master speaks of the 'reverse wheel' where disciples (yogis or devout spiritual practitioners) turn away from worldly affairs in order to dedicate their lives to achieving equanimity and eventually full spiritual awakening.

For this reason, the Soul in Libra is often said to be in a 'resting' phase, as choice is made: to continue on the outer path of worldly pursuits, or to turn inwards and pursue the inner journey of awakening.

It is said that, on a Soul level, Libra has a

foot in both worlds: the material world and the spiritual, as this choice is made.

The theme of transition, passing from one state to another, is therefore also a Libra theme. In ancient Egypt the sign of Libra was associated with the setting of the sun, death, and the beginning of one's journey through the underworld or bardo: the journey of the Soul between worlds: after physical death and before one's next rebirth.

## The Natural Descendant

In one's horoscope, birth is associated with the ascendant, and death is associated with the descendant. If we draw up a horoscope with the first sign of the Zodiac Aries as the natural ascendant then, as Aries opposite sign, Libra is the natural descendant. This symbolizes the descent into the underworld and is the gateway for deeper experiences of death and transformation in Scorpio.

## Libra and Choice

One of the major Libra themes is that of

choice. We can learn much about the esoteric meaning of choice for Libra in *The Labours of Hercules: An Astrological Interpretation* by Alice Bailey.

In Hercules' seventh labour, which pertains to Libra, Hercules is challenged to capture a wild boar. On the way he meets a friend. They take a flagon of wine that doesn't belong to them and get drunk. A fight breaks out in which Hercules ends up killing his two friends.

He then continues on his mission, captures the wild boar, tames it, and steers the exhausted boar down the mountain by holding it's back legs, laughing, and encouraging others to make fun of the suffering animal.

What can we learn from this story, and how does it relate Libra? Hercules quickly forgets his mission and is distracted by worldly activities. (stealing, drinking, fighting, killing).

Here we see the Libra theme of choice between staying focused on our spiritual path and being distracted by worldly pursuits. On a committed spiritual path, Libra reminds us that we must continuously choose spiritual practice over worldly distractions, until we are fully spiritually awakened.

Although he eventually succeeds in his mission to capture a boar, he lacks compassion and is oblivious to the animal's suffering. In addition, following his mission, his teacher says, *"Twice you have slain that which you should love. Learn why."*

What caused Hercules to behave like this? The answers to this question are found deep within the mysteries of Libra. Why do any of us give in to temptation and not always do that which is for the highest and best good of all?

Hercules makes poor choices because he allows himself to be driven by old habits. Hercules is a warrior and a hero. He is trained to fight and kill. We can see in some of his other challenges, especially that of Virgo, that he often resorts to killing first, as a default solution. This is a difficult habit to break.

The reason Hercules was given this challenge in Libra was not only to capture the wild boar, which he did, but also to witness his own unenlightened behavior that comes from his past habits. In other words, it was an opportunity for him to begin to see his own karmic conditioning, which needs to change if he is to pursue a spiritual path to awakening.

The spiritual path of Libra teaches us all just how hard it is to stay focused on our spiritual path. It is not the objects of temptation themselves that are the problem, but our habits: our tendency to repeat old karmic patterns, that pull us off course and lead us away from making significant progress in our journey of spiritual awakening.

## The Libra Glyph

The glyph for Libra is thought by some astrologers to be a rudimentary drawing of a pair of scales.

It has also been pointed out that the modern Libra glyph is often depicted as the Ancient Greek letter Omega above a horizontal line[13]. The horizontal line could represent the horizon while Omega, as the final letter of the Greek alphabet, is often associated with endings.

---

[13] Illustrations of Omega and the Egyptian hieroglyph for Libra can be found online at https://astrology-symbols.com/libra-symbol/

The word Omega also literally means 'great', so the glyph for Libra could be implying that there is a '*great ending*' of some kind. This would not simply be a reference to death, which is an everyday occurrence and in many spiritual and esoteric traditions is thought to lead to rebirth, but is more likely to hint at a 'final' end: the complete end of the cycle of death and rebirth, which happens at the time of full spiritual awakening (enlightenment).

One of the most commonly used Egyptian hieroglyphs for Libra depicts it as a picture of the Sun setting over the earth. As mentioned above this symbolizes the descent of the Soul into the underworld at death.

We can see in much of the Libra symbology that there is a continual theme of a choice between worldly life or a spiritual life, or of some kind of threshold between two worlds. One of the reasons why the deeper esoteric meaning of Libra can be difficult to understand is because for many hundreds of years, the esoteric scriptures were kept secret.

The Greek word *eso* means *within*, so *eso*teric teachings are there to guide us in exploring our inner world, our inner experience, so that we may realize the highest wisdom of enlightenment. They often don't make sense from the perspective of worldly life.

Esoteric spiritual teachings are not there to offer guidance in worldly activities. They are teachings that were originally only given to devout spiritual practitioners: mostly monks, nuns, disciples, and yogis. In other words, spiritual practitioners who had given up worldly concerns to dedicate themselves to spiritual practice until they achieved full spiritual awakening or enlightenment.

To try and understand esoteric teachings from the perspective of our ordinary worldly life, is to take them out of context, and this is where misunderstandings can occur. This is why esoteric scriptures were kept secret for many hundreds of years.

When we look at words such as equanimity, the understanding and meaning shifts, depending on our level of consciousness or spiritual practice. We have an everyday understanding of equanimity, yet there is also an ultimate meaning that can only be understood from higher consciousness.

## The Great End

As we have seen, the deepest esoteric meaning of Libra is *ultimate equanimity*. This can't be understood from our everyday level of consciousness because our everyday consciousness experiences everything in terms of polarity: judging all experience as good or bad; right or wrong.

The deepest understanding of equanimity arises when we are quite advanced in our spiritual path to the point where we have fully transcended duality. At this point, when one is able to rest fully in equanimity, all worldly phenomena are experienced as 'equal' since it is clear that they do not have the power to disturb the natural state of calm abiding. Realizing this deepest spiritual truth is the spiritual path of Libra.

The purpose of any spiritual path is to recognize our innate essence of joy, clarity, wisdom, peace, and compassion but when we live in the polarity of our everyday mind we believe our happiness is dependent upon things outside of us, for example having a good day and not having a bad day.

Breaking the habit of labelling all our experience as good or bad, and practicing mindfulness to return to the pure awareness within which the experience is happening, is an advanced spiritual practice that is designed to cut through the duality of our everyday mind and allow us to glimpse our true nature. This is the applied spiritual practice of equanimity.

The spiritual path of Libra includes the *applied practice* of equanimity, which eventually leads to the actual *experience* of ultimate equanimity, and the *capacity to rest* in our natural state. This spiritual practice eventually leads to enlightenment, which is the end of suffering.

Enlightenment is said to end all suffering, because with it comes the end of the cycle of death and rebirth (samsara). Ultimately the Libra symbol hints at this Great End: the end of all suffering.

# SCORPIO

Scorpio's Symbol of a Scorpion is possibly the most well-known of the Zodiac, but there is more to this symbol than meets the eye. Scorpio is one of the most intense and enigmatic signs of the Zodiac and one which sometimes attracts a lot of negative attention, so it is worth looking more deeply at the symbology of this powerful sign, and why it represents a significant turning point on our Soul's journey.

As we mentioned earlier, in *Esoteric Astrology* the Tibetan Master explains that our Soul begins it's journey in Aries as "a point of light in the mind of God", and then continues through each of the twelve Zodiac signs.

Some soul astrologers believe the soul spends up to *eight lifetimes* in each sign, which gives us a sense of the vastness of our Soul's journey. So the fact of reincarnation and the idea that our soul is progressing through each of the Zodiac signs, like developmental stages, form a fundamental basis for soul astrology.

On our Soul's journey through the Zodiac although at each stage there are important areas of growth, there are also significant transition points, one of which is Scorpio. Scorpio is the last of the signs of crisis[14]. It is in Scorpio that we experience trials and tribulations that force us to confront the illusion of the personality and face up to the reality of our Soul.

Esoterically it is in the sign of Scorpio that personality-Soul fusion happens and completing the lessons of Scorpio prepares the individual to walk the first path of service in Sagittarius. One of these significant Scorpio

---

[14] In *Esoteric Astrology*, the twelve Zodiac signs are grouped together as four signs of preparation, four signs of crisis and four signs of service. Read more *Soul Astrology: How Your Rising Sign Reveals Your soul Path and Life Purpose*.

lessons is around death.

In everyday life most people tend to think of death as pretty final! In mainstream western culture the idea of reincarnation, or that we have any conscious experience following the death of the physical body, is not featured very highly in our collective psyche. Yet this is one of the deepest lessons of Scorpio.

Following the trials of Scorpio the individual knows once and for all, with absolute certainty, that death itself is an illusion, that consciousness remains and cannot die, and that there is an aspect of our consciousness that is eternal. These realizations come through the intensity of experience in Scorpio.

That deep, probing-beneath-the-surface that Scorpios are known for, is exactly what is needed to understand the truth of our reality as beings of love and light.

According to *Esoteric Astrology* Scorpio is a ray four sign. Ray four is the ray of harmony and beauty through conflict, otherwise known as 'the path of artistic living'. The conflict comes as our awareness of our soul grows stronger, and the obsessions and compulsive desires of the personality conflict with the reality of our Soul.

The harmony and beauty comes as one by one our personality compulsions dissolve into the love, light and beauty of our Soul. It is said that one of the highest soul purposes of Scorpio is to embody Divine Love. For this to happen we must already be aware of our Soul light, and allow that awareness to grow within our minds and hearts. This is what happens in Scorpio.

> *"The function of Scorpio on the personality level is to attract those circumstances — especially on the emotional plane of desire — which engage the personality in battle."*
>
> – Alan Oken
> *Soul Centered Astrology*

Anyone with Scorpio Rising, and/or Sun or Moon in Scorpio, is acutely aware of this inner conflict: an inner tug-of-war between the desires of the personality, and the growing awareness of the Soul's presence.

This is why the sign of Scorpio is associated with (at least) three symbols: the scorpion (sometimes spider), the snake (or lizard) and the phoenix (or eagle). These represent the stages on the Soul's journey through Scorpio.

## The Scorpion

The scorpion or spider symbolizes the intense pursuit of illusory egoic desires, purely to feed the lower personality or ego. There is no awareness of, or higher aspiration towards, Soul experience. This is summed up in the personality keynote for Scorpio:

*"Let maya flourish and let deception rule"*

– The Tibetan
*Esoteric Astrology*

## The Snake

Once there is even a glimmer of Soul awareness, this light begins to grow and the individual is henceforth on a path of transformation. Like the snake or lizard shedding it's skin many times over, there will be many, many, layers of personality dissolving away to reveal the light of the Soul. This is the long path of healing and transformation, which leads to the ultimate triumph of Scorpio: the embodiment of Love.

We may also think of the eagle as a symbol of this transition from the second to the third stage of Scorpio's journey. Like the phoenix, the eagle has the ability to soar to the greatest heights (in many native American traditions the eagle represents Great Spirit). Yet in nature eagles still have the predatory nature of the scorpion, which brings a great capacity to focus on their prey.

When the eagle is less focused on captivating external objects of desire to serve the interests of the personality, and focuses on the light of the Soul, then the final transformation into the phoenix begins.

## The Phoenix

The phoenix is a symbol of transformation, reincarnation and re-birth. In mythology the phoenix triumphs over death. There are variations of the story but according to one version, when the phoenix 'dies' she bursts into flames and then 'rises' or is re-born from her own ashes.

This symbolizes the consciousness and life that continues after the death of the physical body. It is the ultimate triumph of Scorpio and is summed up in the Soul keynote for Scorpio:

*"Warrior am I
and from the battle
I emerge triumphant"*

– The Tibetan
*Esoteric Astrology*

Another little-known symbol for Scorpio, is the Dove[15]. The Dove is symbolic of the fully

---

[15] Linda Goodman described three 'stages' of Scorpio (or types of Scorpios) as scorpion, grey lizard and eagle; Alan Oken uses the symbology of scorpion, spider; eagle; and phoenix. Linda Goodman has the eagle as the final stage, while Alan Oken puts the eagle as stage two and the phoenix as the final stage. See Alan Oken's Soul Centered Astrology pp.212-214.

enlightened Scorpio. One who has completed the process of personality-Soul fusion, and is a fully Soul-Centered being. This is the culmination of the lessons in Scorpio and the individual then embodies pure, Divine Love.

If you have Scorpio Rising you may experience some deep crises at times throughout your life, that test your personality to the limit. This is all for good reason. It is through these final tests in Scorpio that your Soul fully awakes.

When the lessons of Scorpio are complete you will emerge renewed like the phoenix rising from the ashes, to continue your Soul's journey through the signs of service: Sagittarius, Capricorn, Aquarius and Pisces.

---

There is also an association between the glyph of Scorpio and the symbolism of the snake shedding it's skin. See pp.119-120 Alan Oken's Complete Astrology (he also describes the symbolism of the Dove on pp.127-128).

# SAGITTARIUS

The Zodiac sign of Sagittarius is associated with truth, freedom, goals, higher knowledge and liberation. It is the sign of the philosopher, and both the spiritual teacher and the spiritual seeker.

The symbol for Sagittarius is the archer, pointing his bow and arrow to the heavens, but this is not your average archer – the archer that represents Sagittarius is also a centaur, half man and half horse.

This conjures up imagery of hunting, seeking, focusing on a target (bow and arrow) and (perhaps more importantly) of 'man' triumphing over his 'lower' animal nature.

## The Glyph for Sagittarius

The astrological glyph for Sagittarius is an arrow, but in some depictions it almost appears to be a *saltire* (an x-shaped or St. Andrew's cross[16]) with an arrow extending from it's upper right arm. This is also very similar to the symbolism of the centaur.

In astrology a cross is symbolic of matter, while the arrow traditionally is symbolic of a bridge between heaven and earth. So even if we do perceive Sagittarius' arrow as an 'x' with an arrow protruding from it, we conjure up the same idea of setting our goals higher than our physical experience and liberating our spirit from the 'imprisonment' of physical matter.

Esoterically the higher soul purpose of Sagittarius is to *uplift humanity through the revelation of truth and wisdom*. With regard to our Soul journey Sagittarius is described as, *a beam of directed, focused Light*.

---

[16] The name Andrew means manly, or brave, and St. Andrew's day is celebrated on November 30th, in Sagittarius season.

The symbolism behind Sagittarius is therefore all about searching: aspiring for something higher, something better, a 'loftier' goal.

In terms of our spiritual journey the sign of Sagittarius is associated with 'liberation'. In the Buddhist tradition 'liberation' is seen as a stage on the path to enlightenment but not full enlightenment itself.

Liberation is said to be the stage at which we are 'liberated' or freed from the conditioning of our everyday thinking. But even once we attain liberation there is farther to go until we reach full enlightenment.

In *Esoteric Astrology*, Sagittarius is described as the stage at which we identify the 'correct goal' which then prepares us for 'discipleship' (walking the path to enlightenment) in Capricorn. This is reflected in the esoteric keynote for Sagittarius:

> *"I see a goal.*
> *I reach that goal*
> *and then I see another"*

> \- The Tibetan
> *Esoteric Astrology*

In the Buddhist tradition this idea of journeying beyond our everyday experience is described in the scripture known as the Heart Sutra, which we mentioned earlier in the chapter on Virgo.

A mantra from the Heart Sutra reads,

*Gate gate paragate, parasamgate bodhi svha*

which, roughly translated, means:

*"Gone, gone, beyond.*
*Gone altogether beyond.*
*Oh what an awakening!"*

On an everyday level our Sagittarian friends can be real go-getters: they can see a goal, focus on it, and hold that focus until they arrive. They can be real achievers in every sense of the word.

Yet the deeper symbolism inherent in Sagittarius implies that, way beyond our ordinary everyday experience, we can discover the greater mysteries of life that lie beyond! Sagittarius arrow points the way, inviting each of us to go, go, go beyond… go way beyond… to enlightenment!

# ♑

# CAPRICORN

The sign of Capricorn is possibly one of the most mysterious of the entire Zodiac. Capricorn is associated with business, finance, ambition, the political sphere, accounting and resource management, yet on a spiritual level Capricorn is also the sign of the initiate and the disciple. It seems that this enigmatic sign is the most earthy and the most spiritual at the same time!

Understandably for such a mysterious sign, there are various symbols used to depict the Zodiac sign of Capricorn: the goat, the sea-goat, the crocodile and the unicorn.

Capricorn is associated in a material sense with ambition, and in a spiritual sense with ascension. Whether we are talking about the material world or the spiritual plane it seems that Capricorn's job is to ascend the heights! As with Scorpio, the different symbols used to for Capricorn represent different stages of consciousness or spiritual awakening.

## The Goat

The goat is one of the earthiest animals imaginable and is perfect to symbolize the material earth-bound aspect of Capricorn. In nature goats live in the most rugged, inhospitable terrain on earth. They are masters of survival. They can climb some of the sheerest inclinations and rocky landscapes with sure-footed certainty, and have the most hardy digestive systems which means they can eat (and get nourishment from) practically anything they find along the way.

This conjures up images of a yogi in a loincloth living in a mountain cave for years, surviving only on light, fresh air and a couple of grains of rice once a week! It speaks to

Capricorn's ability to master physical resources while keeping their attention on the higher (spiritual) purpose. The Goat symbolizes Capricorn as a survivor.

## The Crocodile

In nature crocodiles are masters of conserving energy. They are often mistaken for logs, which is part of their success as predators. Unlike most predators Crocodiles do not chase their prey.

They are more inclined to lie in wait until some unsuspecting zebra comes too close then they will suddenly spring into action, clutching their target in their jaws, and dragging them under the water.

Here we see more Capricorn qualities in action: patience, timing, the ability to remain focused, and precision. Rarely do Capricorns waste anything, especially time, energy and/or money. The symbolism of the Crocodile reflects Capricorn's mastery of physical resources.

## The Unicorn

In addition to the goat and the crocodile, Capricorn is also associated with two mythological creatures: the Unicorn and the Sea-Goat. In some spiritual traditions the Unicorn is seen as a symbol of spiritual realization.

In the myth of the Lion and the Unicorn, the Lion represents Ego, while the Unicorn represents our spiritual nature. The Lion (ego) is defeated when it is pierced *through the heart* by the horn of the Unicorn (spiritual awareness). The symbology here is that our ego dissolves when spiritual awareness awakens our heart. The Unicorn represents the higher, more spiritually aware, aspect of Capricorn.

*"At the foot of the mountain, the goat, the materialist, seeks for nourishment in arid places.*

*The scapegoat on the way up finds the flowers of attained desire, each with its own thorn of satiety and disillusionment.*

*At the top of the mountain the sacred goat sees the vision and the initiate appears.*

*In other writings the symbols are the goat, the crocodile and the unicorn."*

– The Tibetan
*The Labors of Hercules:*
*An Astrological Interpretation*

## The Sea-Goat

The Latin name for the constellation of Capricorn is *capricornus* which means horned goat. It's symbol is that of a mythological sea-goat. The origins of the sea-goat myth have been somewhat obscured by the mists of time, but seem to be associated with ancient Greece.

In Greek mythology the sea goat Pricus was associated with Chronos (Lord of time). In the myth Pricus' children were able to pull themselves onto the land with their two front hooves. However the more time they spent on land the more they became like physical goats.

As they lost their connection to the ocean, they lost their ability to think and speak and became like the animal goat[17].

---

[17] Read the full story in *Capricorn Mythology: The Story Behind The Capricorn Constellation* by Mike Belmont. Online

There are two signs that have this ability to live both on land and in the ocean: Cancer (symbolized by the crab) and Capricorn (our sea-goat). There is something deeply symbolic about this, which could be about our ability to incarnate from spirit into matter and then return to spirit.

In many spiritual traditions the ocean is used as a metaphor to represent the Great Spirit or void from which all matter and life forms arise. This indicates the deep connection that Capricorn has to both the physical realm and our deeper spiritual nature.

## The Capricorn Glyph

In Esoteric Astrology, The Tibetan said that the astrological glyph for Capricorn has never been correctly drawn, because it is the "signature of God".

Certainly the glyph for Capricorn is drawn in a variety of different ways to this day. Many

document at
https://www.gods-and-monsters.com/capricorn-mythology.html

astrologers think it is a symbolic representation of the horned goat with the fishes tail.

However when glyphs are hand-drawn, particularly when they are used as shorthand to save time, there is also the possibility that it becomes a matter of what is convenient, rather than precision.

For example the Capricorn glyph that I find easiest to draw quickly looks like a number seven with a curly tail (see the image at the beginning of this chapter). However there is also another interesting similarity to the Capricorn glyph that intrigues me.

In Tibetan Buddhist traditions the Tibetan syllable 'ah[18]' is said to represent the highest spiritual attainment: the 'top' of the spiritual mountain.

*"All the teachings of Buddha come down to Ah"*

– Lama Zopa Rinpoche
in the documentary *Mystic Tibet*

---

[18] The syllable would be equivalent to the letter A, while the sound would be 'ah'.

The Tibetan syllable 'ah' looks remarkably like the astrological glyph for Capricorn. Especially when rotated by 90°. Since the Tibetan syllable is possibly older[19] than our current Capricorn glyph it may be more accurate to say that the glyph for Capricorn is like the Tibetan syllable 'ah' rotated by 90°!

Tibetan syllable AH

Tibetan syllable AH rotated 90°

Maybe the original glyph for Capricorn was something more like the Tibetan syllable ah, in the sense that it represented our spiritual essence, and subsequently became distorted over time as we lost sight of our true nature.

A glyph that is symbolic of our spiritual essence would certainly be more in accord with the highest spiritual purpose of Capricorn.

---

[19] The Bön tradition of Tibetan Buddhism is said to be over 17,000 years old.

# AQUARIUS

Aquarius is symbolized by the *water carrier* which gives us an indication of the deeper meaning of this enigmatic sign. Indeed the word *aquarius* is Latin for water (aqua) carrier, so we can particularly take note that the symbolism inherent in this sign is more about the carrier, or vessel, and not the water itself.

There is something important about Aquarius being a container, vessel, or vehicle. In *Esoteric Astrology* it is said that through Aquarius' pitcher flow the *dual waters of love and life*, which again is hinting something about Aquarius' role in flowing energy.

People born under this sign often make awesome networkers. There is something innate in Aquarius' understanding of circulating energy. In Medical Astrology, while Leo rules the heart, it is Leo's opposite sign Aquarius that rules the *circulation* itself.

It seems that on many levels, Aquarius plays an important role in the creation and maintenance of channels through which the dual energies of 'love' and 'life' can flow throughout humanity.

The 'dual waters' are a way of describing our Soul's energy, by drawing attention to two qualities. In exploring this it is important to understand that they aren't separate, but are actually two qualities of the same thing. To illustrate this point, in Tibetan scriptures they often use the example of the Sun.

We all experience the Sun's light, and heat, but we can never separate the two. They are both essential aspects of the Sun's energy. Sometimes we can place our attention on the light and don't notice the heat so much. Like on a sunny winter's day.

At other times we might focus on the heat

and not notice the light so much. Like on a hot summer's night. But both qualities are always ever-present within the Sun.

Likewise with Aquarius we are talking about the dual energies of Love and Life (prana or life-force energy) that originate in our Soul and that we can flow, emanate, or radiate, through our heart for the benefit of all. They are two qualities of the same thing: our Soul's light or essence.

In meditation, and through our daily activities, we can notice how our heart energy is flowing. We can see for ourselves how sometimes it feels like Love, and at other times it feels like Life but however we experience it in any moment, it is always the same thing: our Soul's Essence.

Aquarius (together with Gemini and Virgo) is one of the few signs that is symbolized by a human form. This gives us another hint at one of the spiritual purposes of Aquarius.

Aquarius is the sign of the humanitarian, and in *Esoteric Astrology* Aquarius is associated with the higher group consciousness of humanity. So now we are beginning to see a picture emerge of a sign that is highly symbolic of *the evolution of human consciousness* through our ability to circulate the dual waters of love and life throughout humanity.

There is much in the mythology of Aquarius that refers to this association with flowing water. In Greek mythology Aquarius is associated with the myth of Ganymede, a young boy who was captured and enslaved to become the 'water-bearer' to Zeus, yet the association of Aquarius with flowing water appears to be even older than that.

## The Glyph for Aquarius

In *The Aquarius Symbol*[20], Stefann Stenudd writes that the ancient Babylonians associated Aquarius with their God *Ea* which meant *"The Great One"*. We'll come back to the meaning of 'great one' in a moment but just in terms of the name Ea, some scholars think it could possibly be, "a derivation from the West-Semitic root *hyy* meaning *life* in this case used for *spring*, [and] *running water.*[21]"

---

[20] Online article at:
https://www.helloastrology.com/aquarius/aquarius-symbol/
[21] From https://en.wikipedia.org/wiki/Enki

This is interesting because once again it brings us to an image of flowing, or running water (or the running water of life). This shows us how the association between running water and Life itself goes back to ancient times, as it has been long recognized that running water is essential for Life itself to exist.

However, on a deeper level, although water may be a basic necessity for Life to exist, it is often not so obvious that love is also essential for Life to be sustained. Reports of infants left in orphanages in the 19th century[22] showed that although their physical needs were met, they often did not survive without love.

The glyph for Aquarius, *two* wave-like lines, are therefore symbolic of the essential 'dual' waters of love *and* life that are needed for us to not only survive, but to thrive, and evolve in consciousness.

In Alice Baileys book *The Labours of Hercules: An Astrological Interpretation*, the labour that is associated with Aquarius is one of cleansing the Augean stables. In this myth Hercules is challenged to clean the royal stables of a King,

---

[22] https://eipmh.com/they-could-not-live-without-the-love/

which had never been cleaned before and so were caked in the stench and filth of years of accumulated dung!

Hercules' challenge was to clear them in one day, a task that was thought to be impossible. There were two rivers flowing nearby, and Hercules accomplished the task by simply re-directing the rivers, which flushed out the stables.

In the symbology of Aquarius the continuous theme of flowing water emerges, and always with a human involved: possibly acting as an agent of change or awareness. Not only do we have a theme of flowing energy, but there is always some human involvement, a *conscious awareness*, with the ability to choose and direct the flow of energy.

## The Great One

Earlier we noted that the Babylonian God Ea was associated with Aquarius and that his name meant "The Great One". In terms of spiritual truth, the 'Great One' (also known as "Great Spirit" in some native American traditions) is not a separate individual but is actually Oneness itself: the great Universal Mind of Divinity within which we all exist, and from which all manifest phenomena emerge. This leads us to the highest spiritual purpose of Aquarius.

As the fixed air sign, Aquarius is a sign of the mind (all air signs are about Mastery of Mind). One of the highest spiritual purposes of Aquarius is to go beyond the workings of lower mind and ego, to realize the presence and reality of the Universal Mind of Oneness.

Once there, the ebb and flow of Life itself will be known, as it is seen how the waters of Love and Life continuously emerge from, and dissolve into, the ocean of One.

The symbolism of Aquarius therefore carries deep and significant meaning about Divine oceanic consciousness (the water) being expressed in the form of Love and Life, through the 'vessel' known as the body of humanity (the carrier).

## PISCES

The symbol for Pisces Symbol is the fishes: two fish swimming in seemingly opposite directions. This immediately tells us that Pisces is a sign of duality, yet it is important to note in the symbology, that the fish are never separate: there is always a bond, a thread of some kind, connecting the two.

Why two fish specifically, and not two of any other animal? The answer is probably lost in the mists of time but is likely to be about the symbolism of water and the sanctity of water. The fact that on Earth it is water that gives and sustains life, and also that water is a metaphor for our spiritual nature, Divinity, and oceanic consciousness. In other words, we arise from an ocean of consciousness within which we spend our lives, just like fish spend their lives in physical water.

Pisces is the mutable water sign and is associated with oceanic consciousness. We can relate to the two fish as aspects of our individuality swimming through that ocean of consciousness: one fish symbolizing our body and the other our Soul.

In astrological symbology, water represents our emotions. All water signs (Cancer, Scorpio and Pisces) are mastering emotions on some level. Pisces is very connected to the astral realm: the realm of emotions, psychic impressions, the imagination and the subconscious.

The sign of the fish is also used in Christian symbolism: Christ chose His disciples from fishermen. He performed the miracle of the loaves and the fishes. Modern day Christians also use the sign of the fish. Interestingly, the Christian faith itself was established during the beginning of the *Great Astrological Age of Pisces*[23].

## The Pisces Glyph

The glyph for Pisces consists of two semi-circles facing away from each other, joined by a band.

It is said that the two 'fishes' are permanently joined together by a 'silver cord' which is sometimes called the *sutratma* or *thread of life*.

The sutratma is a reminder that we are never separate but that we are connected by the thread of life which runs through all our hearts.

*"The Sutratma, the thread of life, is anchored in the heart. It comes directly from the Monad, reflected through the soul, and is fixed in the heart center at the right-hand side of the body.*

*It is reflected through that etheric center to the physical heart and into the bloodstream, which, as you know, is the purifying stream which carries the energy of life to every part of the body.*

---

[23] See the chapter on Leo for more about the Great Astrological Ages.

*While the lifeblood is pumped correctly through the body and is kept free of poisons, the physical body displays all its ability and accuracy of movement and expression.*

*So, too, the connecting body, the astral-emotional body and the mental body are dependent on the life thread, the Sutratma, for their existence and correct function."*

– Benjamin Creme,
from *The Antahkarand*[24]

There is a strong heart connection in Pisces which shows that through the *Sutratma* the individual thread of life, *we are all connected* through the heart center.

For this reason Pisces is also associated with the sacred heart of humanity, which is the potential for all human hearts to beat as one as we uplift and sustain each other in our collective spiritual awakening.

It is through the sutratma heart connection that we awaken others, by awakening ourselves. The more we awaken as individuals, the more we contribute to what is known as the

---

[24] Online article at:
http://www.esoteric-philosophy.net/antak.html

Great Enlightenment, or Great Awakening, in which the whole of humanity awakens.

In many spiritual traditions our spiritual journey is described as a *path of the heart*. It is through the heart that the energy of suffering is transformed into spiritual energies such as universal love and compassion.

Esoterically it is said that the final death happens in Pisces. This would be the final death of ego (after many 'false' deaths) where once and for all our illusory ego dissolves into the ocean of consciousness.

When we finally recognize ourselves as that ocean, we are truly at one with all that is. So in Pisces we have the culmination of a heart journey (of transforming human emotions) that began in Cancer, and completes with the 'death of ego' in Pisces.

*"The happiness of the drop is to die in the river."*
– Sufi proverb

The glyph of Pisces represents this journey: in the two semi-circles we can see an illusion of separation. They appear to be separate, going in opposite directions. Yet all the time we can see the connecting thread. We can also see that once the two halves turn to face each other, the result will once again be a complete circle.

Esoteric Astrology teaches that all suffering is the result of the *illusion of separation*. The story of our apparent separation and return to wholeness, represented by Pisces Symbology, is one of overcoming human suffering as we return to the wholeness of universal love and compassion.

# MORE BY THIS AUTHOR...

## *FREE - Your Essential Guide To Soul Astrology*

A simple introduction to the basics of Soul Astrology. Available to purchase at RuthHadikin.com or get it free by subscribing to Ruth's free newsletter, *"Life's Greatest Adventure"*.

## *Soul Astrology: How Your Rising Sign Reveals Your Soul Path and Life Purpose*

Discover your Soul Path and life purpose for this incarnation. A potentially mind-blowing read, Soul Astrology can show you *WHAT* you came here to do AND *HOW* you'll do it! Available at RuthHadikin.com

## *The Complete Foundations of Soul Astrology*

Going even deeper into the Soul-Centered meaning of the 12 Zodiac signs, this book also introduces the Soul-Centered meaning of the planets and houses. A priceless companion on your spiritual journey. Available at RuthHadikin.com

## *Rising Sign Series*

A series of short reads - one for each Soul Sign (Choose yours based on your Rising Sign).

- Personality vs Soul

- Soul Recognition

- Personality and Soul Expressions of your Soul Sign

- Your Unique Soul Meditation
Available at RuthHadikin.com

## *Soul Sign Explorations*

Deeper insights into the twelve Zodiac Signs from Aries through to Pisces, from an esoteric and Soul-Centered perspective. The teachings of The Tibetan in Esoteric

Astrology are compared and contrasted with contemporary Tibetan Buddhist teachers for deeper understanding of the essence of what the Tibetan was trying to convey. Available at RuthHadikin.com

### *Soul Sign Videos*

Ruth Hadikin reads about each Soul Sign and gives additional commentary. Watch the trailer at RuthHadikin.com

### *Learn to Meditate*

In this short Kindle book, Ruth introduces different meditations, some active, some sitting, and a quick-start meditation, so everyone can practice this ancient art of spiritual awakening. Available at RuthHadikin.com

## *Living Soul Astrology - Online Course and Community*

Written and video lessons, meditations, and an online community to support you in going deeper on your journey with Soul Astrology. Full details at RuthHadikin.com

# ABOUT THE AUTHOR

Ruth Hadikin BSc. graduated with a first class honors degree (summa cum laude) in midwifery. She has studied spiritual and esoteric subjects since she was 19 years of age, integrating her wisdom with experience gained from her own spiritual practice and worldwide travel.

Her defining talent is bringing deep insight, clarity and simplicity to complex subjects - in particular *Esoteric Astrology* and the teachings of The Tibetan through the work of Alice Bailey.

Ruth has travelled extensively in the UK, Ireland, Spain, USA, Australia, Kenya, Egypt, India, Nepal and Tibet. She has lived in England, Scotland, Spain and the USA. She specializes in supporting you on your own greatest adventure: using Soul Astrology to explore your Soul Path and Life Purpose.

Websites:
RuthHadikin.com
Astrology-Symbols.com

eMail: Ruth@RuthHadikin.com

9 780099 555936 3